Contents

Book Map

Theme	Reading text type	Reading skills
1 Education, Teaching and Learning	Textbook articles	• Revision
2 Daily Life, Nature … or Nurture?	Magazine articles Magazine interview	• Confirming precise meaning • Finding the main point of an article • Identifying negative prefixes
3 Work and Business, SOMething to Live For	Magazine articles	• Recognising supposition
4 Science and Nature, Forecasting the Weather	Magazine articles	• Finding the main information in an active sentence • Looking for evidence in a text
5 The Physical World, Black Gold	Encyclopedia article	• Finding the main information in a passive sentence • Understanding internal definitions
6 Culture and Civilization, Twenty-Six Civilizations	Web pages	• Finding the main information in a complex sentence – participle joining • Researching on the Internet – search engines and indexes / FAQs
7 They Made Our World, Preserving Food	Web search results Hyperlinked text	• Finding the main information in complex sentences with *that* / *which* / *who*, including embedded clauses • Using hyperlinks • Understanding the writer's attitude – stance words
8 Art and Literature, Dickens and *David Copperfield*	Biography Text extract	• Making inferences about background knowledge
9 Sports and Leisure, Predict and Provide	Tables Graphs Pie charts	• Understanding tables and figures
10 Nutrition and Health, Love Your Heart	Leaflets	• Revision

Skills in English

Reading

Level 3

Terry Phillips

Garnet
EDUCATION

Published by
Garnet Publishing Ltd.
8 Southern Court
South Street
Reading RG1 4QS, UK

This edition first published 2004

ISBN 1 85964 792 8

British Library Cataloguing-in-Publication Data
A catalogue record for this book is available from the British Library.

Production
Project manager: Richard Peacock
Editorial team: Nicky Platt, Lucy Thompson
Art director: David Rose
Design: Mark Slader
Illustration: Beehive Illustration/John Dunne
Photography: Corbis/Bettmann/L. Clarke/
                    Rob Lewine/Ariel Skelley, Digital Vision,
                    Image Source, Photodisc, Pixtal

Google™ is a trademark of Google Inc.

Every effort has been made to trace the copyright holders and we apologize in advance for any unintentional omissions. We will be happy to insert the appropriate acknowledgements in any subsequent editions.

Printed and bound
in Lebanon by International Press

Introduction

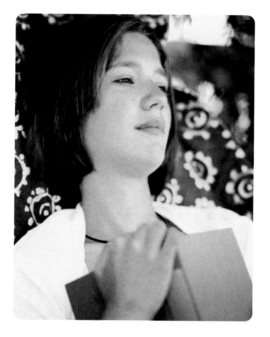

THIS COURSE IS THE READING COMPONENT of Level 3 of the *Skills in English* series. The series takes students in four levels from Lower Intermediate to Advanced level in the four skills, Listening, Speaking, Reading and Writing.

The reading component at each level is designed to build skills that help students survive in an academic institution where reading research is wholly or partly in English.

This component can be studied on its own or with one or more of the other components, e.g., Listening and Writing.

The course is organised into themes, e.g., *Science and Nature, Art and Literature*. The same theme is used across the four skills. If, therefore, you are studying two or more components, the vocabulary and structures that you learn or practise in one component will be useful in another component.

Within each theme there are four lessons:

Lesson 1: *Vocabulary*
In the first lesson, you revise words from the theme that you have probably learnt already. You also learn some new words that you need to understand the texts in the rest of the theme.

Lesson 2: *Reading*
In this lesson, you practise skills that you have learnt in previous themes.

Lesson 3: *Learning new skills*
In this lesson, you learn one or more new skills to help you with reading.

Lesson 4: *Applying new skills*
In the final lesson, you use your new skills with another reading text. In most cases, the texts in Lessons 2 and 4 have a similar structure, so you can check that your skills have improved.

In this theme you are going to read about learning and teaching.

Lesson 1: Vocabulary

You are going to learn some of the vocabulary you will need to understand the texts.

A Write a red word in each space to complete the dictionary entries.

_____ **1** the part of the brain where information is kept; *I have a good ~* **2** a particular piece of information; *I have no ~ of my childhood before the age of five.*

_____ keep in the memory; not forget; *I can't ~ where I put my keys.*

_____ lose from the memory; not remember; *Don't ~ to call me later.*

_____ the organ of the body that stores information and controls activity; *There is nothing wrong with his ~. He just doesn't work hard enough.*

_____ look again at information you have studied before; *Are you going to ~ for the test this weekend?*

B Complete the text with a green word in each space. Make any necessary changes.

We can divide most subjects at college or university into two types. Some subjects involve a lot of _____, for example, medicine. A person who wants to become a doctor must know a lot of information about the human body to be successful. Other subjects involve a lot of _____, for example, physical education. A person who wants to become a PE teacher needs to be able to play a lot of different sports and to be able to teach them. (Sometimes we use a different word to talk about teaching a skill. We call it _____.)

Some subjects involve _____ and _____. A person who wants to become a brain surgeon, for example, needs to know all about the brain, but he or she also needs to be able to use very complicated machinery.

At the end of the period of teaching or training, we must _____ a learner's knowledge or skill. We must find out if the learner has _____ a good level. It is quite easy to _____ knowledge with a written test or an interview. It is much harder to _____ skills, like ability in sports or in teaching itself.

brain *(n)*

forget *(v)*

memory *(n)*

remember *(v)*

revise *(v)*

achieve *(v)*

assess *(v)*

knowledge *(n)*

skill *(n)*

training *(n)*

C Discuss these points about the information in Exercise B.

1 Are you studying a knowledge subject or a skills subject? Or does your subject involve knowledge *and* skills?

2 How do the teachers assess your knowledge of the subject or your skills in the subject?

3 Why is it harder to assess skills than knowledge?

Lesson 2: Reading

A You are going to read a chapter from a book for teachers.
1 Read the title of the chapter.
2 What do the words *teaching* and *learning* mean?

B Read the introduction and the topic sentences from the text (in green).
1 What do you think the main idea is?
2 Make a list of questions you want the text to answer.

C Read the text on pages 4 and 5 of the Reading Resources book.
1 Check your idea in Exercise B1.
2 Find answers to your questions in B2.

D This text does not have paragraph headings, but it could have. Choose a heading from the yellow box for each paragraph.

E Choose the best summary of the text.

1
Teaching is not the same as learning. You need to think carefully about what you are going to teach before you go into the classroom.

2
Learning is not the same as teaching. Every lesson should have a learning aim and a teaching aim. After the lesson, you must think about what you have taught and what the students have learnt.

3
Teaching does not equal learning. A teacher must think about the learning aim of a lesson and decide if the students have achieved the aim by the end.

F Discuss these questions.
1 Was this a Presentation, Practice or Production lesson?
2 What was the main aim?
3 Was it achieved for you?

CHAPTER ONE

Teaching and Learning

In this book, you are going to learn a great deal about teaching. However, before we concentrate on teaching, we must think about learning. In this first chapter, we will study the words 'teaching' and 'learning'. If you remember the exact meanings of these words, it will help you before, during and after each lesson.

Teaching means helping people to learn, or telling or showing people how to learn.

The meaning of the word 'learning' changes according to what you are trying to learn.

Learning only needs one person, the learner.

Teaching is about helping people to learn.

It is difficult to write a learning aim from the definition of learning above.

| Teaching aims … or learning aims? |
| Teaching and learning |
| The key questions |
| What does 'teaching' mean? |
| What does 'learning' mean? |
| Which is more important – teaching or learning? |
| The learner |

Lesson 3: Checking skills

A Find 12 words connected with teaching and learning in the Wordsearch box. You can read →↓↘.

B Choose five words from the Wordsearch. Make one sentence with each word.

C These sentences are true or probably true. Find evidence in the text on pages 4 and 5 of the Reading Resources book. Write the line numbers in the spaces provided.

1 This text is for teachers. (   )

2 Self-study can mean studying with a book or a CD-ROM. (   )

3 Distance training can mean studying through the Internet. (   )

4 You can learn without anyone teaching you. (   )

5 You can teach without anyone learning. (   )

6 The writer thinks teachers should plan lessons. (   )

7 This text is not just for language teachers. (   )

8 There are three main types of lesson. (   )

9 Presentation lessons have new information in them. (   )

10 The writer thinks practice makes you better at things. (   )

a	m	e	m	o	r	i	s	e
e	a	c	q	u	i	r	e	n
a	s	s	e	s	s	g	s	p
i	c	c	v	p	k	r	t	e
b	e	h	a	v	i	o	u	r
o	e	k	i	z	l	t	d	u
u	f	w	m	e	l	e	y	l
i	m	p	r	o	v	e	h	e
a	g	b	n	m	u	e	j	s
k	n	o	w	l	e	d	g	e

D What should a teacher think about when planning a lesson?

1 Make a list of questions.

2 Check with the text.

E Here are some aims for lessons in different subjects. Which question in Exercise D above does each one answer?

1 For students to understand the rules of the past simple question forms. (English)

2 For students to learn about a famous ruler of their country. (History)

3 For pupils to become fluent in the '7 times' table. (Maths)

4 For students to learn how to deal with angry customers. (Management training)

5 For students to practise a scene from a play. (Drama)

F Read the Skills Check Reminders. Tick (✓) the skills you have practised so far in Lessons 2 and 3.

Skills Check

Reminders

When you read a text, you must …

- skim for the main idea.
- skim for the topic of paragraphs.
- read for an established purpose.
- make inferences – 'read between the lines'.
- transfer information, e.g., text to outline.
- react to a text.
- apply ideas to real-world situations.
- apply information to new situations.
- distinguish fact from opinion.
- recognise the writer's point of view.
- recognise comparisons.
- follow a narrative.
- identify missing information.

Lesson 4: Applying skills

A You are going to read an article about language learning. Number these items in order of usefulness to you in learning English.
- ___ grammar rules
- ___ pronunciation rules
- ___ pairwork
- ___ group work
- ___ listening and repeating
- ___ role plays
- ___ homework / assignments
- ___ reading

B Read the title of the article. Do you understand what it means?

C Read the introduction. The text describes two types of language learning. What are they?

D Read the topic sentences.
1 What do you think is the main idea?
2 Make a list of questions you want the text to answer.

E Read the text on pages 6 and 7 of the Reading Resources book.
1 Check your idea in D1.
2 Find answers to your questions in D2.
3 What does the title of the article refer to?

F Look at Table 1. Work in pairs.
Student A
1 Find information in the text to complete the language acquisition column. Tick the features that are mentioned.
2 Tell your partner about your findings.

Student B
1 Find information in the text to complete the language learning column. Tick the features that are mentioned.
2 Tell your partner about your findings.

L1 *and the* LAD

How do we learn a language? It is a difficult question to answer, partly because it is not really one question, but two. The first question is: *How do we learn our first language?* The second question is: *How do we learn a second or foreign language?*

Why do we need to separate the questions?

Linguists use special words to talk about L1.

Does a child have to try to learn his or her mother tongue?

Are all children fluent in their mother tongue?

What about language *learning*?

Is there really an LAD?

Table 1: Features of language acquisition and learning

features	language acquisition	learning
actual teaching		
automatic learning		
factual correction		
correcting grammar		
correcting pronunciation		
grammar rules		
pronunciation rules		
focus on form		
focus on communication		

In this theme you are going to read two articles about how people develop.

Lesson 1: Vocabulary

You are going to learn some of the vocabulary you will need to understand the articles.

A Discuss these questions, which use the red words.

1 Which of these people have the most effect on a *child*'s attitudes and behaviour?
- the *parents* (father or mother?)
- other *adults* (which ones?)
- other *children* (which ones?)

2 Which of these people have the most effect on an *adult*'s attitudes and behaviour?
- the *parents* (father or mother?)
- the *husband* or *wife*
- the *children*
- other *adults* (which ones?)

B Read the text.
1 Complete the text with a green word in each space.
2 Complete the table with information from the text.

A group of Americans was asked the question: What are the most important factors that _____ the way your life turns out? Nearly all of the people asked (93%) said, 'The biggest _____ is hard work.' The next biggest response (51%) was, 'It's all decided by God.' Exactly half of the respondents said, 'It's your _____, particularly how your parents _____ you up.' Thirty-one percent said, 'It's based on _____. It's the things you _____ from your parents.' Just under a fifth (19%) said, 'Your _____ isn't important. Your _____ aren't important. It's all a matter of chance.'

Table 1: Responses from a group of Americans

The way that life turns out ...	
___ **a** depends on how hard you work.	
___ **b** is decided by God.	
___ **c** is a result of your environment.	
___ **d** is based on genetics.	
___ **e** is a matter of chance.	

C What do you think are the most important factors affecting the way life turns out? Work in groups. Conduct a survey with other people in your class. Number the factors (a–e in Table 1) 1–5, where 1 = the most important. Record your results in a table.

adult *(n)*

child/ren *(n)*

husband *(n)*

parent *(n)*

relationship *(n)*

response *(n)*

wife *(n)*

affect *(v)*

bring up *(v)*

environment *(n)*

factor *(n)*

genes *(n)*

genetics *(n)*

inherit *(v)*

Lesson 2: Reading

(A) Which of these features did you inherit from your parents?

1 the colour of your hair
2 the colour of your eyes
3 your height
4 your weight
5 your intelligence
6 your likes and dislikes
7 your health (good or bad)
8 your behaviour

(B) You are going to read an article from a science magazine.

1 Read the title. Do you think this article will talk about the points in Exercise A?
2 Read the introduction. What do you think now?

(C) The article contains information about the points in Exercise A.

1 How can you find the information in the article quickly?
2 Follow your ideas and try to find the information in one minute. The article is on pages 8 and 9 of the Reading Resources book.
3 How many paragraphs did you read? Find the topic sentence from each paragraph – on the right – and tick (✓) it.
4 Does the information agree with your ideas in Exercise A?
5 Why did you not read all the paragraphs?

(D) Read the topic sentences from the article that you did not tick again. What information do you expect to find in each paragraph?

(E) Read the article on pages 8 and 9 of the Reading Resources book again. Deal with new words as you read. Then close the Reading Resources book and tell your partner what information each paragraph contained.

(F) What conclusion did the article reach? Discuss in pairs then check with the article.

Nature ... or Nurture?

WHY HAVE YOU GOT BROWN EYES and not blue? Why do you weigh 68 kilogrammes and not 60? What accounts for your level of intelligence? Why do you behave the way you do? Most people think they have inherited their eye colour, but what about the rest? Even psychologists and geneticists do not agree about the rest.

There has been a debate about this issue for many years.

It is easy to find an answer with plants.

Nowadays, we can even find an answer with animals.

We are unable to use either of these approaches with human beings.

We cannot generalise from the results with plants or cloned animals to say anything useful about human beings.

So, where can we look for evidence about the effect of nature and nurture on people?

Through these studies and other research, scientists have discovered many interesting facts.

Factors like intelligence and personality are less easy to attribute to nature or nurture.

What about negative traits?

Lesson 3: Learning new skills

A We can often say the same thing in different ways, but we sometimes need to change the form of the main content word.

1 Write a suitable noun or adjective in each space.

2 Check with the text on pages 8 and 9 of the Reading Resources book.

   a It's in my <u>genes</u>.   It's _____.

   b I <u>inherited</u> it.   It's _____.

   c It's from my <u>environment</u>.   It's _____.

   d Why do I <u>behave</u> this way?   What accounts for my _____?

   e The way we <u>bring up</u> a child …   A child's _____ …

   f … affects the way it <u>develops</u>.   affects its _____.

   g I am <u>susceptible</u> to certain diseases.   I have a _____ to certain diseases.

   h How does nature <u>affect</u> a person?   What is the _____ of nature on a person?

   i Nature and nurture make you the <u>person</u> you are.   Nature and nurture produce your _____.

   j What did you <u>conclude</u> from your studies?   What was your _____ from your studies?

   k Some research suggests that children of criminals <u>tend</u> to be criminal.   Some research suggests that children of criminals have criminal _____.

B What do these words and abbreviations mean? They are all from the article in Lesson 2.

> clone DNA genes nurture trait

1 Try to explain the meaning.

2 Read Skills Check 1.

3 Look up any words you are not sure of in a dictionary.

C These sentences are not true or probably not true. Find evidence in the article on pages 8 and 9 of the Reading Resources book. Write the line numbers in the spaces provided.

1 The writer thinks scientists understand the role of nature and nurture. ( )

2 There is a nature or nurture debate about plants. ( )

3 There is a nature or nurture debate about animals. ( )

4 Plant and animal research helps us understand nature and nurture in humans. ( )

5 Twins always get the same diseases. ( )

6 Environment has no effect on intelligence. ( )

D What is the quickest way to find the main point in a magazine article?

1 Think of a way.

2 Read Skills Check 2 and check.

E Look at these words from the article.

> impossible immoral unethical unlikely

1 What do the words have in common?

2 Find some more words with the same patterns.

Skills Check 1

Confirming precise meaning

You can usually guess the **general meaning** of a new word from context. But you often need the **precise meaning** to really understand an article. Check specialised terms in a dictionary.

Skills Check 2

Finding the main point of an article

Where can you find the main point of a magazine article? In the introduction? In the topic sentences? In the main body? No. The main point is normally in the final paragraph – the conclusion. Read the introduction first, then the conclusion, then go back and read the topic sentences.

Lesson 4: Applying new skills

Ⓐ We found some negative words in the article in Lesson 2.
1. Read the Skills Check, then cover it.
2. What is the missing prefix in each case?
   a ____legal
   b ____responsible
   c ____agreement
   d ____able
   e ____ethical
   f ____possible
   g ____caring
   h ____moral
   i ____order
   j ____social
   k ____likely

Ⓑ You are going to read another article about nature and nurture.
1. Read the title. Do you remember the point about this in the article in Lesson 2?
2. Read the introduction. What structure do you expect in this article?
3. What should you read next?
4. Look at the article on pages 10 and 11 of the Reading Resources book. Find out in one minute what Professor Morgan believes.
5. There is a secondary, or inset, article, on pages 8 and 9. What is the main point of that part?

Ⓒ Read the main article.
1. Find and circle any specialised words. Look them up in a dictionary.
2. Find and underline any words with negative prefixes. Can you guess the meaning from context?
3. List any pieces of information about identical twins that you knew already.
4. List any new pieces of information.

Ⓓ Follow the procedure in Exercise C with the secondary article.

Ⓔ Which piece of information from this whole theme do you find the most surprising? Why?

Are Identical Twins the Key to Understanding Nature and Nurture?

This week, *Science Today* talks to Professor Andrew Morgan, a geneticist, about his work and the nature or nurture debate.

In this theme you are going to read two articles about working conditions.

Lesson 1: Vocabulary

You are going to learn some of the vocabulary you will need to understand the articles.

(A) Read the text.

1 Find and underline the red words.

2 Write a red word in each dictionary definition.

The advertisement has generated quite a lot of applicants for the job of Trainee Manager. I have to evaluate them, look at their strong points and their weak points, and then select three of them for a trial period of three months. After the trial period, I will decide which ones to employ. It is quite a long process, but it is the best solution to the problem of getting new staff. In this company, we have an acronym for the process – we call it GESD – which we pronounce like *guest* because we are bringing a guest into the company.

1 _____ choose an action after thinking about something

2 _____ work out the good and bad things about an idea, a person, etc.

3 _____ a formal word for *choose*

4 _____ an answer to a problem

5 _____ a number of stages in a particular activity

6 _____ a number of letters that represent, e.g., an organisation or a process

7 _____ make, produce

acronym *(n)*

applicant *(n)*

decide *(v)*

evaluate *(v)*

generate *(v)*

imagine *(v)*

process *(n)*

select *(v)*

solution *(n)*

colleague *(n)*

flexible *(adj)*

overtime *(n)*

promotion *(n)*

salary *(n)*

secure *(adj)*

security *(n)*

(B) Look at the advertisements. Write a green word in each space. Make any necessary changes. Then check with a dictionary.

Do you want a job with a high _____?

Do you want quick _____? Are you prepared to work long hours without _____ pay? Then join us as a Trainee Manager and get on the fast track! _____ begins at $500 per week. At the end of your six months' training, you become an Assistant Manager, with _____ to Manager within the next six months. Your job is then _____. Stay with us for the rest of your life if you want.

Would you like to decide:

- **when to start work in the morning?**
- **when to finish work in the afternoon?**
- **how many hours you work?**

Would you like to be able to change your working hours at short notice? For a job with _____ working hours, phone Superstores – the supermarket for women who work and have a family. E-mail us now at www.superstores.com and start a new working life with friendly _____ in a clean, healthy environment.

Lesson 2: Reading

A Read the factors that might be important if you are considering a new job.

  1 Number the five most important factors for you (5 = most important).
  2 Ask four other people for their most important factors. Record the results.
  3 Combine your results. Produce a table showing the order for the top five factors.

It is important to me to ...	Me	1	2	3	4	Total	Order
a have a secure job.							
b have an interesting job.							
c do something worthwhile.							
d have a good salary.							
e be able to organise my own work.							
f learn new skills.							
g have a chance of promotion.							
h work in a clean, healthy place.							
i work for a successful company.							
j work for a boss I respect.							
k have flexible working hours.							
l be recognised for my good work.							
m be able to do paid overtime.							
n have few problems with colleagues.							

B You are going to read a newspaper article about factors in employment.

  1 Read the headline on the right. What do you think the article is about?
  2 Read the first paragraph. What do you think now?
  3 Read the final paragraph. What do you think now?

C Look at the article on pages 12 and 13 of the Reading Resources book. Read the topic sentences. What information do you expect to find in each paragraph?

D Read the whole article. Check your ideas from Exercises B and C.

E Which of these statements are true or probably true, from the information in the article? Write the line numbers in the spaces provided.

  1 Men and women in the UK have very similar needs at work. (   )
  2 Men and women in my country have very similar needs at work. (   )
  3 All of the results of the survey are in line with management theories. (   )
  4 The results of the survey should be of interest to managers in the UK. (   )
  5 The people who took part in the survey told the truth about their needs. (   )
  6 People are not interested in the salary when they apply for a job. (   )

F Which piece of information in the article do you find the most surprising? Why?

An Interesting Job Is Better than a Well-Paid One

Both women and men would rather have an interesting job than a highly paid one. That is the conclusion of researchers, following a recent survey of public opinion. The survey involved more than 3,000 men and women across the United Kingdom.

The results of this survey should make some managers think again about the way they manage. Interesting, worthwhile jobs seem to be more motivating than well-paid ones.

Lesson 3: Learning new skills

A Here are the factors as written on the graph on page 13 of the Reading Resources book. Make a full question in each case.

Example: *Is it important for you to … work for a boss you respect?*

1 boss I respect
2 chance of promotion
3 clean, healthy place
4 few problems with colleagues
5 flexible working hours
6 good salary
7 interesting job
8 new skills
9 organise own work
10 paid overtime
11 recognised for my good work
12 secure job
13 something worthwhile
14 successful company

B You must understand what each noun and phrase in a text refers to.

1 Read the Skills Check Reminder.
2 Match the nouns and phrases that refer to the same thing in the article in Lesson 2.

a	work satisfaction	1	apparently
b	a say in	2	control over
c	hardly rated	3	manager
d	questioned	4	not important
e	finding	5	poll
f	survey	6	possibly
g	presumably	7	result
h	perhaps	8	surveyed
i	boss	9	an interesting job

C Read this part of the article from Lesson 2 again.

> The most striking example was in rating the importance of working for a boss that you respect. Women put this factor in fourth place, whereas men put it tenth. Perhaps this is because women are often not respected by their (male) managers.

1 Which finding from the survey is this part about?
2 What is a possible reason for this finding?
3 Read Skills Check 2 and check.
4 Can you give another supposition about this finding?
5 Find more suppositions in the paragraph beginning: *Although men and women agreed …*
6 Can you give another supposition for each one?

Lesson 4: Applying new skills

(A) Match the words to make phrases from the article connected with work.

1 flexible		**a** company
2 secure		**b** job
3 good		**c** overtime
4 paid		**d** salary
5 successful		**e** skills
6 new		**f** working hours

(B) You are going to read another survey about attitudes to work.
1 Read:
  a the headline.
  b the first paragraph.
  c the final paragraph.
2 Make a list of questions you expect the article to answer.

(C) Study the graph from the article. Does it answer any of your questions from Exercise B?

Figure 1: Managers' and workers' assessment of own needs

Managers and Workers Just Need SOMething to Live For

Do workers and managers have the same needs at work? A recent study suggests that they do. The study, which involved 30 managers and 300 workers in the Wessex area, was conducted by the University of Wessex. The results show striking similarities between the needs of managers and those of their workers. However, they also show that both managers and workers are unable to accurately assess the needs of the other group.

So just remember SOM when you think about SOMebody else at work. They probably have the same needs as you.

Assessment of own needs

(Bar chart showing percentage for factors: interesting, secure, worthwhile, lot of money, independent, liked, high status, good time. Legend: workers (black), managers (grey). x-axis: percentage 0–100.)

(D) Read the article on pages 14 and 15 of the Reading Resources book. Check your ideas from Exercises B and C.

(E) Find four suppositions in the article. Can you think of other possible reasons for any of the findings?

(F) How can managers provide SOM for their workers?

In this theme you are going to read two articles about forecasting the weather.

Lesson 1: Vocabulary

You are going to learn some of the vocabulary you will need to understand the articles.

A Discuss these questions. They use the red words.
 1 How many kinds of *climate* can you name?
 2 What is the world's biggest *desert*? What do you know about it?
 3 Name 10 *living things*.
 4 Name five *plants* in English.
 5 Where would you expect to see a *polar* bear?
 6 Do you live in a *tropical* area? Explain your answer.

B Read the text and look at the table.
 1 Write a green word in each space. Make any necessary changes.
 2 Think of a definition for each green word.

Most scientific work involves similar processes (see Table 1). It starts with a question. Then scientists _____ an answer. They do an experiment, or they _____ what happens in nature. They _____ data. This usually involves _____ something, e.g., temperature. Finally, they _____ that the prediction was correct or incorrect.

climate *(n)*

desert *(n)*

living thing *(n)*

plant *(n)*

polar *(adj)*

tropical *(adj)*

collect *(v)*

conclude *(v)*

measure *(v)*

observe *(v)*

predict *(v)*

C Copy words from Table 1 into the correct place in Table 2.

Table 2: Some scientific verbs and nouns

verb	noun
predict	
observe	
collect	
measure	
conclude	

D Discuss these questions. They use the green words.
 1 What can you *predict* accurately?
 2 How can you *observe* animals?
 3 How can you *collect* personal data about people, e.g., *name, age, address*?
 4 How can you *measure* temperature?
 5 Peter was driving at 150 kph and he crashed. What might you *conclude* in this case?

Table 1: The scientific process

process	example
Question	*Why do clouds sometimes produce rain?*
Prediction	*Clouds will only produce rain if they have small pieces of ice in them.*
Observation	*Some clouds produce rain when they are very low.*
Data collection, e.g., *measurement of temperature*	*The temperature of low rain clouds is too high to have pieces of ice in them.*
Conclusion	*Some clouds will produce rain even if they do not have small pieces of ice in them.*

Lesson 2: Reading

A How did people predict weather hundreds of years ago? Think about:

sky   clouds   animals   records

B You are going to read an article about the history of weather forecasting. Look at the first paragraph, the topic sentences of the main body and the final paragraph.

1 What is the article about?

2 What is the main point of this article?

C Look again at the topic sentences from the main body of the article. Which sentence below do you expect to follow each topic sentence?

1 They could also say where the weather was going to, since it was widely known that the wind carried the weather from one location to another.

2 For example, in England and many other countries in the Northern Hemisphere, there is a famous saying:

3 They were particularly interested in shooting stars.

4 We could call it *here and now* forecasting.

5 We are going to consider how accurate weather forecasting was in the days before modern data-collecting devices.

6 In 1592, an Italian named Galileo invented a thermometer that could record temperature accurately.

D Read the text on pages 16 and 17 of the Reading Resources book. Check your answers to Exercises B and C.

E What does the writer mean by these kinds of forecasting?

1 here and now

2 repetition

3 there today, here tomorrow

F Look again at the pieces of weather lore in the article.

1 What does each one mean?

2 Do you have any of these sayings in your country?

3 What other sayings do you have?

Jan 1st, 1760 Cold and wet today.

Jan 2nd Much colder but no rain or snow.)

HOW CAN WE PREDICT THE WEATHER TOMORROW IN A PARTICULAR PLACE? Throughout history, Man has tried to perform this useful task, and has succeeded, with greater and greater accuracy. Today, weather forecasts for the next 24 hours can be very accurate, and even five-day forecasts from the Meteorological Office are right more often than they are wrong.

In this, the first of two articles, we are going to look at how it all started.

In the 5th century BCE, the Ancient Greeks were interested in natural events that happened in the atmosphere, like clouds and rain.

We now call a lot of early forecasting *weather lore.*

These pieces of weather lore predicted the weather in one place in the next six to 12 hours.

Of course, until instruments existed for accurately recording temperature and atmospheric pressure, the written records were along the lines of 'warmer and wetter than yesterday'.

By the middle of the 18th century, therefore, people with a thermometer and a barometer could predict their local weather for the next 12 hours with some accuracy.

So, by the beginning of the 20th century, weather could be accurately recorded in one place, at least in terms of temperature and pressure, and that data could be transmitted quickly to another place. The age of *there today, here tomorrow* forecasting had arrived.

Lesson 3: Learning new skills

A Find the words in the blue box in the text on pages 16 and 17 of the Reading Resources book.
1 What can you work out about the meaning **from context**?
2 What is the **precise meaning** in each case?

atmosphere	seagull
meteor	pack up
hail	bear in mind
hemisphere	principle
old wives' tale	irrelevant

B You must find key information quickly in long sentences. The key information often answers the question, *who did what*?
1 Who did what in the sentences in the yellow box? Try to find the information in each sentence in less than five seconds.
2 Read Skills Check 1 and check your method.
3 What does the word *that* refer to in sentences a, b and d in the box?

a In 1592, an Italian named Galileo invented a thermometer that could record temperature accurately.
b By the 17th century, people were making temperature observations that led to more accurate *repetition* forecasting in many places.
c In 1643, Galileo's pupil, Torricelli, invented the barometer and measured atmospheric pressure.
d In the 5th century BCE, the Ancient Greeks were interested in natural events that happened in the atmosphere, like clouds and rain.

C Imagine you received this assignment.

'People could forecast the weather accurately before 1850.' Discuss.

The word *Discuss* in an assignment means *give evidence **for and against** the statement.*
1 From the information in the reading text in Lesson 2, do you think this statement is true, false, or partly true?
2 Read Skills Check 2. Follow the advice.

Skills Check 1

Finding the main information in a sentence (1)

Sentences in English usually have the pattern S(ubject), V(erb), O(bject). Find the SVO quickly in each sentence and you have found the main information. But you often have to hunt for the SVO.
Examples:

1 In 400 BCE, Aristotle wrote a book that was called …	S = Aristotle V = wrote O = a book
2 It contained his thoughts about rain, cloud, mist, snow …	S = It (the book) V = contained O = his thoughts

Always look for the SVO in a long sentence. Circle the S, underline the V and box the O.
Use these clues to find the SVO quickly.
1 Ignore short phrases at the beginning of a sentence up to a comma.
2 Ignore everything after the word *that*.
3 Ignore information after prepositions.
4 Look for a new S after *and, but, or*. If there is no S, the subject must be from the last sentence.
Then go back and see if you can understand the extra information, especially *when* things happened.

Skills Check 2

Looking for evidence in a text

When we do reading research, we are often looking for **evidence for** and / or **against** a particular point.
Make a table and write notes in each column while you are reading.

for	against
there was weather lore from observing the sky and the clouds	people could not transmit the data to other places

Lesson 4: Applying new skills

A Look at the pictures.
  1 What is the connection between all the items?
  2 How many can you name?

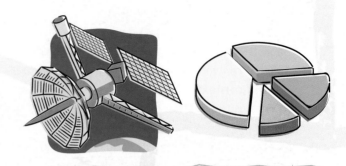

B You are going to read a second article about weather forecasting. Look at the introduction, topic sentences from the main body and the conclusion.
  1 What is the article about?
  2 What is the main point of the article?
  3 What is the article going to talk about in each of the main body paragraphs?

C Scan the article on pages 18 and 19 of the Reading Resources book. Check your answers to Exercises A and B.

D Read the article again. Use the ideas from the previous lesson to find the SVO in long, complicated sentences.

E Imagine you have received this assignment.

> 'Weather forecasting is now a science rather than an art.' Discuss.

Make a table and record information from the text for and against this statement.

F What will the weather be like here tomorrow?

There are two stages to modern weather forecasting. The first stage is collecting information. The second stage is predicting changes in weather, based on the information collected. The first stage is a very well-developed science. To some extent, the second stage is still an art.

There are many ways that information is collected nowadays about weather conditions.

Collection devices at sea and on the land measure a number of aspects of weather.

Observations at ground level are only half of the story when it comes to forecasting weather.

The radiosondes are tracked from the ground, which gives a measurement for wind speed at the altitude of the balloon.

The final, and most recent, data-collection instrument is the satellite.

The World Meteorological Organization (WMO) has 150 member countries that receive data from 10,000 land stations, 7,000 ships and buoys, hundreds of balloons and several satellites.

Once the data for current weather around the world has been collected and plotted on a weather map, forecasters try to predict what will happen in the future.

Weather forecasting is now extremely accurate, especially for the next five days. However, meteorologists still do not fully understand what causes local weather conditions, and even modern computers cannot do all the necessary calculations fast enough to predict perfectly. As a weather forecaster once said, 'With my computer, I can predict tomorrow's weather with 100% accuracy, but it will take me one week.'

In this theme you are going to read some encyclopedia entries.

Lesson 1: Vocabulary

You are going to learn some of the vocabulary you will need to understand the entries.

A Discuss these questions about your country. Some of them use the red words.

1 Which countries are your *neighbours*?
2 Which *border* is the longest?
3 What is the *population* of your country? Is it rising or falling?
4 What is the *area* of your country?
5 What is the *climate* of your country?
6 What are the most important *natural features* of your country?
7 What are the main *industries* in your country? Which products do those industries produce?

B Read the text about 'black gold'. Choose a green word for each space. Make any necessary changes.

_____ (or *oil*, as it is commonly called) is a fossil ____, like coal. This means that it was _____ millions of years ago at the same time as fossils were made. Petroleum is used to generate electricity and to make many products that are part of the modern world, like _____. However, petroleum will not last forever. One day it will _____ and we will have to use other sources of _____, like the sun or the wind.

In ancient times, people sometimes found oil on the _____ of the Earth, but about 150 years ago people started _____ holes in the ground near surface oil to find the underground _____. Gradually, _____ began to understand which kind of rock formation often contained _____ oil, and they could tell oil companies where to dig their _____.
Oil is so valuable that some people call it 'black gold'.

C Can you name:

1 another fossil fuel?
2 another source of energy?
3 another product that is made from petroleum?
4 a large oil company?
5 a large oil producer?

D Discuss these questions.

1 Does your country produce oil? If so, where? How much per annum?
2 Does your country import oil? If so, from where? How much per annum?
3 Which country is the biggest producer of oil in the world?
4 Which country is the biggest importer of oil in the world?
5 Do you think we should reduce petroleum consumption? Why (not)?

area *(n)*

border *(v)*

industry *(n)*

natural feature *(n)*

neighbour *(n)*

population *(n)*

drill *(v)*

energy *(n)*

form *(v)*

fuel *(n)*

geologist *(n)*

petroleum *(n)*

plastic *(n)*

run out *(v)*

source *(n)*

surface *(n)*

underground *(adj)*

well *(n)*

Lesson 2: Reading

A What is the relationship between each pair of words from Lesson 1?

1 last	run out	**4** fuel	energy
2 underground	surface	**5** drill	dig
3 petroleum	oil	**6** form	formation

B You are going to read about petroleum. Find the subject, verb and object, if any, in these complicated sentences from the text.

1 Petroleum, or *oil,* as it is commonly called, is a naturally occurring hydrocarbon.

2 In addition, petroleum is an important raw material, or basic substance, in several chemical industries, including the manufacture of plastics, textiles and medicines.

3 As more decaying organisms were deposited on top, the pressure increased.

4 However, in most cases, the oil became trapped beneath an impermeable layer of hard rock.

5 Five thousand years ago, the Egyptians sealed their pyramids with pitch, which is the sticky remains of natural petroleum.

6 When they invaded Spain, the Arabs carried the art of distilling petroleum into Western Europe.

7 By the 1600s, the distillation of petroleum produced lubricants that reduced the friction of turning wheels.

8 The invention of the internal combustion engine shortly afterwards ensured a ready market for the main product of the new technology.

C Work in groups of eight.

1 Choose one research question each from the green box.

2 Do you know anything about this subject already? Make some notes.

3 Research the topic. Find information to answer your question in the encyclopedia article on pages 20 and 21 of the Reading Resources book. Make a summary of the information. List any new words in the section that you read.

4 Work with other people who researched the same question. Compare your summaries and word lists.

5 Report back to the other people in your group. Take notes to answer the other research questions.

6 Read the other sections of the text. How good were the summaries you heard?

D In the blue box, you will find definitions of some of the new words from pages 20 and 21 of the Reading Resources book.

1 Look at the list of words you made in Exercise C3 above. Try to find a definition for each of your words.

2 Look again at the text. Check your ideas.

3 Define your words to the rest of your group.

---

a How was petroleum formed?

b What did people in ancient civilizations use petroleum for?

c Who is 'The Father of Petroleum'? How did he get the title?

d What were the first products made from petroleum?

e When did people start drilling for petroleum?

f How do geologists find petroleum nowadays?

g What is 'wildcatting'? How did it get its name?

h When will petroleum run out?

- tiny creature
- the sticky remains of natural petroleum
- boiling a liquid then condensing the vapour
- medicine for rubbing on damaged skin
- dropping a complex sensor down an exploratory well
- exploring for oil on a small scale
- costing less to produce than the value of the product

Lesson 3: Learning new skills

Ⓐ What can you remember about oil? Discuss:
Formation   History   Exploration

Ⓑ The article on pages 20 and 21 of the Reading Resources book is full of technical terms.
1 Read Skills Check 1.
2 Find and underline the words and phrases from the blue box in the text.
3 Which of these words and phrases is defined immediately or later in the text?
4 Can you guess from context the meaning of each of the other words?

hydrocarbon	potential
raw material	sensor
woven reeds	seeping
lubricant	systematic
patent	pioneer
contaminated	reservoir

Ⓒ Study this sentence from the text.
Petroleum is found on or below the surface.
1 Find the subject, verb and object (if any).
2 Read Skills Check 2. Check your ideas.

Ⓓ You must decide quickly whether a sentence is active or passive.
1 Read this section of the text. Find all the verbs. Circle the active verbs, box the passive verbs.
2 Find the subjects of active verbs and the objects of passive verbs.

The first well was dug in Germany in 1857, but the one that caught public attention was drilled near Oil Creek in Pennsylvania in 1859. It hit a reservoir of light oil like kerosene. The invention of the internal combustion engine shortly afterwards ensured a ready market for the main product of the new technology. In 1908, oil was discovered in Iran, and during the next 40 years, discoveries occurred all over the Middle East, in Iraq, Kuwait and other Gulf States. After the Second World War, the development of the petroleum industry in the region led to massive economic expansion.

Ⓔ Find and underline five more passive verbs in the text on pages 20 and 21 of the Reading Resources book. What is the object in each case?

Looking for internal definitions

Writers often define technical terms immediately, or somewhere else in a text.

Defined ...	Example
after *is / are*	*Petroleum **is** a naturally occurring hydrocarbon.*
after *or*	*transformed **or** changed ...;*
after *In other words*	*viable. **In other words, will it cost less ...?***
after *which*	*with pitch, **which** is the sticky remains of natural petroleum*
with another word or phrase	*... the sea was filled with tiny organisms. **These creatures** ...*
in brackets	*a hydrocarbon **(a chemical compound that ...)***
by explanation	*an impermeable layer, a layer that **did not let liquid through***
with the origin	*... wildcatting **because** oilmen had to remove wild cats ...*

Finding the main information in a sentence (2)

We know that English sentences are usually **SV(O)**. A sentence with this pattern is **active**.
Example:

S	V	O	extra
People	**find**	*petroleum*	*on the surface.*

However, there is a common form of sentence that is **OV(S)**. A sentence with this pattern is **passive**.
Examples:

O	V	S	extra
Petroleum	**is found**	*(by people)*	*on the surface.*

In passive sentences, the subject comes after the preposition *by* or does not appear at all.
Use these clues to find passive sentences quickly:
1 Part of *be* comes before main verb, e.g., *is*
2 The main verb = past participle, e.g., *found*

Notes:
Regular verbs have the same form for the past tense and past participle.
You can often guess the infinitive of an irregular verb from its past participle.

Lesson 4: Applying new skills

Ⓐ Match the words to make phrases.

1 oil	combustion
2 raw	field
3 internal	gas
4 wide	material
5 natural	oil
6 exploratory	range
7 light	technology
8 new	well

Ⓑ What, in the text in Lessons 2 and 3, was / were:
1. filled with tiny organisms?
2. covered by fine sand?
3. transformed into petroleum?
4. trapped under impermeable rock?
5. sealed with pitch?
6. contaminated by oil?
7. extracted from wells?
8. distilled from petroleum?
9. patented by Abraham Gessner?
10. dug in 1857?
11. invented in 1860?
12. discovered in 1908?
13. removed before small wells were dug?
14. developed after the Second World War?

Ⓒ You are going to read more entries from the encyclopedia article about petroleum.
1. Read the words in the green box. They all come from the encyclopedia entries. Can you guess what any of them means?
2. Look at the text on pages 22 and 23 of the Reading Resources book. Find the definition of each word in the text.
3. How can you define the phrases in the blue box?

reservoir	enhance	irrecoverable
unviable	inject	viscous
tapped	refining	vaporise
crude	fraction	bitumen

enhanced oil recovery
crude oil
fractional distillation

Ⓓ Choose one of the research questions in the purple box. Make a summary of the information from the text.

Ⓔ Look at the illustrations. Answer these questions.
1. Which country is the largest producer of oil?
2. How many Gulf States are in the top 12 producers?
3. Where are the largest reserves of oil?
4. What are the total reserves in the Middle East?
5. When will Kuwait run out of oil, according to the information in the tables?

a Why is enhanced oil recovery necessary?
b How does water injection enhance oil recovery?
c How does steam injection enhance oil recovery?
d What happens during fractional distillation?

In this theme you are going to read web pages about civilizations.

Lesson 1: Vocabulary

You are going to learn some of the vocabulary you will need to understand the web pages.

A Find pairs of red words. Explain the connection.

B Read the text.
1 Box the subject and underline the verb in each long sentence.
2 How many civilizations have appeared?
3 How many survive?
4 How can we classify a civilization?

Professor Arnold Toynbee, the British historian, said that 21 civilizations have appeared in the history of Man. Eight of these civilizations still survive, including the Islamic Civilization, the Western Civilization, the Far Eastern Civilization and the Hindu Civilization. Other writers say that the number of civilizations is 26 or 27.

But what exactly is a civilization? How can we recognise it? Various writers have suggested that any civilization is distinctive in one or more of the elements in Table 1. In other words, we can classify a civilization according to its distinctive art, science, religion, etc.

C Study the examples in Table 1.
1 Write a green word in each space.
2 Think of another example for each element.

Table 1: Elements of a civilization

_____	e.g., *new transport methods, such as the wheel*
science	e.g., *discoveries in maths, physics, etc., such as Pythagoras' Theorem*
_____	e.g., *new ideas on right and wrong, such as 'an eye for an eye'*
_____	e.g., *new political ideas, such as democracy*
_____	e.g., *new ways of growing things or raising animals*
_____	e.g., *new ideas on worship, such as the idea of one God*
_____	e.g., *music, art, literature*
_____	e.g., *important buildings, such as the pyramids*
leisure	e.g., *sports and games*
industry	e.g., *new ways of making things, such as heating clay to make pots*

D Discuss the questions.
1 Which civilization are you part of?
2 What is distinctive about your civilization? Make a list of ways in which your civilization is different from another civilization you are familiar with.
   Example: *The system of law is different.*

bride *(n)*

ceremony *(n)*

groom *(n)*

marriage *(n)*

marry *(v)*

reception *(n)*

relative *(n)*

wedding *(n)*

architecture *(n)*

agriculture *(n)*

government *(n)*

law *(n)*

religion *(n)*

technology *(n)*

the arts *(n)*

Lesson 2: Reading

Ⓐ Look at the quiz about ancient civilizations.
1 Do the quiz.
2 Check your answers with the information on pages 24–29 of the Reading Resources book.

Ⓑ You are going to do some research into the Egyptians and the Sumerians.
Work in pairs.
1 Find information about one of the civilizations each. Make a list of new words as you read. Look for internal definitions or check the precise meaning with a dictionary.
Student A: The Egyptians.
Student B: The Sumerians.
2 Exchange information to complete Table 1. Explain the meaning of new words as you go.

Ⓒ Look at the texts about the Egyptians and Sumerians again. Test each other on finding the SV (O or Adj) of long active sentences.

How much do you know about ...
ANCIENT CIVILIZATIONS?

A Number these ancient civilizations in order.
The Chinese
The Egyptians
The Greeks
The Indus Valley
The Romans
The Sumerians

B Which of the civilizations above invented / discovered ...
- democracy?
- heated baths?
- musical notation?
- paper?
- the plough?
- the sailing boat?

Table 1: Classification of civilizations – Egyptians and Sumerians

civilization number	1	2
name	Egyptian	Sumerian
origin		
start		
end		
duration		
main area		
religion		
a technology		
d science		
v agriculture		
a architecture		
n the arts		
c law and government		
e leisure		
s industry		

Lesson 3: Learning new skills

A Identify these words connected with civilizations.

rel_____ sci_____ gov_____
adv_____ agr_____ lei_____
tech_____ arch_____ ind_____

B Read the sentences from Lesson 2 in the green box. Find the second verb in each sentence.
  1 What form is the verb in, in each case?
  2 What is the subject of each verb?
  3 Read the Skills Check and check your ideas.

The Ancient Egyptians were the first people to domesticate animals, making the cat into a house animal and the donkey into a working animal.

The Egyptians built the first sail boats, made from reeds that were woven together.

C Find more examples of sentences with a present participle or a past participle in the texts about the Egyptians and the Sumerians. In each case, work out the tense and subject of the original verb.

D How can you find information quickly on the Internet?
  1 Discuss in pairs.
  2 Do some research:
    Student A: Read Skills Check 2.
    Student B: Read Skills Check 3.
  3 Explain the skills point to your partner.

E Imagine that you are researching advances in science in ancient civilizations.
  1 Which web page are you going to look at first on page 27 of the Reading Resources book?
  2 Which part of the website are you going to look at first on page 26 of the Reading Resources book?

F How could you improve your search in Exercise E?

Skills Check 1

Finding information in a sentence (3)

We can use a non-finite clause to join two related sentences.
Examples:
1 **Second sentence = active**
  The Ancient Egyptians were the first people to domesticate animals.
  ***They made** the cat into a house animal.* =
  *The Ancient Egyptians were the first people to domesticate animals, **making** the cat into a house animal.*
2 **Second sentence = passive**
  The Egyptians built the first sail boats.
  ***It was made** from reeds that were woven together.* =
  *The Egyptians built the first sail boats, **made** from reeds that were woven together.*

Notes:
In the final sentence, the second verb is a **participle**, either **present** (e.g., *making*) or **past** (e.g., *made*). There is no information about tense – present, past, future – and no information about the subject. However, you can work out the subject and the tense from the rest of the sentence.

Skills Check 2

Researching on the Internet (1)

Web pages are indexed by **search engines**. In other words, you can search for information on a particular topic and get a list of web pages. Use the **index of web pages** to decide which pages to jump to (**Example:** page 27 of the Reading Resources book).

Skills Check 3

Researching on the Internet (2)

Some **websites** have an **index of the information** on the site. Use the index to choose which parts of the site to visit.
(**Example:** page 26 of the Reading Resources book).

Lesson 4: Applying new skills

Ⓐ Solve the clues. Find the hidden word that links them all.

1 chemistry, biology, physics										
2 pleasant sounds										
3 a group of people who decide what a country should do										
4 growing crops, raising animals										
5 a system for deciding if an action is right or wrong										
6 the worship of God or gods										
7 an example of architectural advance (Sumerian)										
8 painting, sculpture										
9 novels, poetry, drama										
10 the opposite of 'work'										
11 organised games, often in teams										
12 making things										

Ⓑ Imagine that you are researching advances in ancient civilizations, as in Lesson 3. Look quickly at the web pages on China and the Romans in the Reading Resources book.
1 Which section(s) are you going to read? Decide quickly.
2 Read the section(s) you chose and check your ideas.

Ⓒ Find these participles in the long sentences on the relevant web pages. What was the subject and the original verb in each case?

Indus Valley   ending; producing; showing; specialising
Ancient Greece   developing; giving; living; including; winning; including
China   isolated; destroying; existing; born; using; choosing; going
Romans   called; carrying; meaning

Ⓓ In Lesson 2, you completed a table about the Egyptian and Sumerian civilizations. Research the other civilizations in the Reading Resources book. Complete a table about them.

In this theme you are going to do some Internet-type research into food preservation.

Lesson 1: Vocabulary

You are going to learn some vocabulary you will need to do the research.

A Find a red word for each dictionary definition. Check with a dictionary if you are not sure.

_____ thing made for a special purpose

_____ test something to check an idea

_____ create by thinking

_____ person who creates by thinking

_____ something created by thinking

_____ room for doing experiments

_____ things needed for a particular activity

_____ document that says only the named person can make or sell an invention

_____ device for sending and receiving electrical signals

B Read the text.

1 Complete the text with a green word in each space. Make any necessary changes.

2 What does each of the words in italics refer to?

3 What, according to the text, are these things: **bacteria, influenza, antibiotic, flu, typhoid**?

4 Why, according to the text, do we keep things in a refrigerator?

One of the greatest advances in the history of Man is too small to see without a microscope. *It* was discovered by chance by a British doctor and scientist, Alexander Fleming, in 1928. Fleming was working in his laboratory, trying to find a _____ to treat the _____ influenza (or flu), *which* killed more than 20 million people worldwide in the early 1920s.

Fleming noticed that one of the plates *that* he was using for research had no _____ on *it*. This was very unusual. _____, *which* are tiny organisms, are inside every living thing, including the food *that* we eat. *They* are also in the air around us, and _____ anything if you leave *it* in the open air. Some bacteria are useful, but many are harmful and produce _____, including typhoid, tuberculosis and plague.

Fleming investigated further and found the _____ *that* was stopping the growth. He called *it* penicillin. *It* was the first antibiotic, which means *it* fights _____. Fleming, *who* served in the First World War as an army doctor, realised immediately the possible benefits of the _____. When soldiers were wounded, army doctors could often treat *their* wounds but *they* could not stop the _____ from _____, *which* was often fatal. In addition, if _____ methods, like keeping food in a refrigerator, failed to prevent _____ growing, penicillin could fight the _____ *that* resulted.

device *(n)*

experiment *(v)*

invent *(v)*

invention *(n)*

inventor *(n)*

laboratory *(n)*

materials *(n)*

patent *(n)*

telegraph *(n)*

bacteria *(n)*

disease *(n)*

drug *(n)*

food preservation *(n)*

infect *(v)*

infection *(n)*

substance *(n)*

C The text in Exercise B mentions one method of food preservation. What other methods can you name?

Lesson 2: Reading

A You have received an assignment from your tutor.

1 Read the assignment on the right.

2 What words could you type into a search engine on the Internet?

3 Choose the best phrase from the words in the white box below. Explain your answer.

> main ways
> modern life
> food preservation
> preserving food
> the history of food

Greenhill College

Faculty: Food Sciences   Semester 3

Assignment 4

Food preservation is an important part of modern life. However, until quite recently, most food could not be kept for long periods.

Find out the main ways of preserving food. Then research the history of **salting** for food preservation.

B You have typed your words into a search engine and received the list at the bottom of this page.

1 Which of these sites are you going to visit? In which order?

2 Which of these sites will you not visit? Why not?

C You find a site with the questions in the green box. Which question are you going to click on first? Why?

D Go to pages 30 and 31 of the Reading Resources book. Find the answers to the questions you chose in Exercise C. Make notes of the information. Follow any links.

- Why does food go bad?
- How can you stop food going bad?
- When did people first discover food preservation?
- Why did people need new methods of preserving food?
- Who are the important people in the history of food preservation?
- What about modern methods of food preservation?
- Is all food safe nowadays?

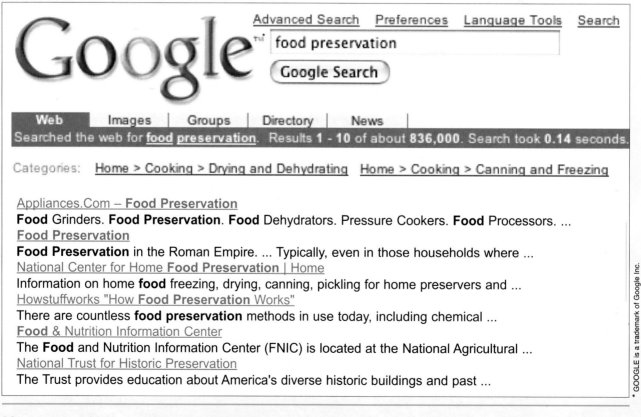

Advanced Search   Preferences   Language Tools   Search

Google™ food preservation

(Google Search)

Web | Images | Groups | Directory | News |

Searched the web for <u>**food preservation**</u>. Results **1 - 10** of about **836,000**. Search took **0.14** seconds.

Categories: <u>Home > Cooking > Drying and Dehydrating</u> <u>Home > Cooking > Canning and Freezing</u>

<u>Appliances.Com – **Food Preservation**</u>
Food Grinders. **Food Preservation**. **Food** Dehydrators. Pressure Cookers. **Food** Processors. ...
<u>**Food Preservation**</u>
Food Preservation in the Roman Empire. ... Typically, even in those households where ...
<u>National Center for Home **Food Preservation** | Home</u>
Information on home **food** freezing, drying, canning, pickling for home preservers and ...
<u>Howstuffworks "How **Food Preservation** Works"</u>
There are countless **food preservation** methods in use today, including chemical ...
<u>**Food** & Nutrition Information Center</u>
The **Food** and Nutrition Information Center (FNIC) is located at the National Agricultural ...
<u>National Trust for Historic Preservation</u>
The Trust provides education about America's diverse historic buildings and past ...

* GOOGLE is a trademark of Google Inc.

Lesson 3: Learning new skills

A How does salting preserve food?

B Many words in the texts in Lesson 2 are in blue.
1 What does this mean?
2 What should you do when you see a blue word in a sentence?
3 Read Skills Check 1 and check your answers to Exercises B1 and B2.

C Read the answers to the first two questions on page 30 of the Reading Resources book.
1 Which hyperlinks did you follow?
2 Which ones did you not follow? Why?

D Study these sentences from Lesson 2.
a *The main problem with food is bacteria, **which occur naturally in all food**.*
b *Two people **who stand out in the history of food preservation** are Nicholas Appert and Clarence Birdseye.*
1 What is the subject of *occur* (a)?
2 What is the subject of *stand out* (b)?
3 Where does the *who* clause end (b)?
4 Read Skills Check 2 and check.

E Can you remember / work out how each sentence continues? Make some notes, then check with the text on pages 30–33 of the Reading Resources book.
1 But sometimes, the bacteria are hidden dangers that …
2 The food will be reinfected by new bacteria, which …
3 No doubt, at first people ate food that ….
4 The Lapps, who … dried reindeer meat …
5 Sailors who … often ran out of meat, which …
6 Nicholas Appert is the man who …, which ….
7 Illnesses that … are still a major health issue.
8 Other methods aim to kill the bacteria that …
9 Roman soldiers received money that ….

Using hyperlinks

Words in texts on the Internet are often in **blue**. These are **hyperlinks**. If you click on a blue word, you will go to **another text** with more information. This is a powerful research tool, but you can get lost!

Follow this advice to use hyperlinks more efficiently:
1 Do not click on a blue word just because it is there. Only click if you need to know more about the particular topic.
   Example:
   You are researching the history of canning and Napoleon is hyperlinked. You probably don't need to click on this.
2 After clicking on a blue word, scan the text to see if it is relevant. If not, click BACK in the browser to go back.
3 If one hyperlink leads to another, etc., click BACK several times to return to the first location.

Finding information in a sentence (4)

Sometimes, sentences have extra information after ***which***, ***who*** or ***that***. These clauses can come:

1 at the end of the sentence.
   Examples:
   *The main problem with food is bacteria, **which occur naturally in all food**.*
   *Some people say there are certain Native American tribes **who used to keep a kind of stew cooking constantly**.*
   Note: The subject of the ***which*** / ***who*** clause is the object of the first verb.

2 in the middle of the sentence.
   Examples:
   *If you leave the food for a long time, the bacteria **that are already in the food** multiply.*
   *Two people **who stand out in the history of food preservation** are Nicholas Appert and Clarence Birdseye.*
   Note: The ***that*** / ***who*** clause comes between the subject and its verb.

Lesson 4: Applying new skills

A Read the sentences in the blue box. They are from the texts in Lesson 2.

1 What word or phrase is missing from each sentence?

2 What is the function of each word or phrase in the sentence?

3 Read the Skills Check and check your ideas.

4 Check with the texts on page 30 of the Reading Resources book.

B You are going to do some more research for another assignment from the Food Sciences Faculty.

1 Read the assignment.

2 Work in pairs:

Student A: Research canning

Student B: Research freezing

As you do your research, make a list of the hyperlinks you follow. If a link is not useful to you, put a cross beside the link.

3 Explain the science and history of your method to your partner.

Greenhill College

Faculty: Food Sciences   Semester 3

Assignment 5

Primitive societies could not preserve food because they did not understand the science of food preservation.

Do some research into the history of EITHER **canning** OR **freezing**. Explain the science behind the method.

C During your research for Exercise B, did you read about any of the following? Why (not)?

• cell division
• vacuum
• vinegar
• rehydrating
• evaporation

---

a You cannot see the bacteria in food, _____, even when there are millions of them, unless you have a microscope …

b _____, the higher the temperature, the quicker food goes off.

c _____, you must kill all of the bacteria …

d Primitive tribes did not know how to store food, and therefore _____ suffered the consequences.

e _____, at first people ate food that had gone off, and fell ill or even died as a result.

f _____ there are certain Native American tribes who used to keep a kind of stew cooking constantly.

g _____ these stews existed for 20 or 30 years.

h _____ that people dried food in primitive societies.

i Salting was also used from an early date to preserve food, although this process also affects the flavour of food, _____.

Skills Check

Understanding the writer's attitude

Writers often show their attitude to information in a text by adding extra words or phrases. When you see the words and phrases below, stop and think. *How does the writer feel about this information?*

Word or phrase	Writer's attitude
Of course / *Clearly /* *Naturally*	This is true.
No doubt / *Presumably*	This is probably true.
Generally speaking	This is usually true.
There is evidence	This may be true.
Some people say / *There are stories that /* *It is said that*	This may be a myth.

In this theme you are going to read a short biography of Charles Dickens and extracts from one of his most famous works.

Lesson 1: Vocabulary

You are going to learn some vocabulary to help you understand the texts.

A Think of your favourite story.

1 What is the *plot* of the story – in three sentences?

2 What is the most exciting or interesting *event* in the story?

3 What is the *theme* of the story – love, adventure, problems in society …?

4 What is the *origin* or *source* of the story? Is it traditional, or do you know the name of the writer?

B Read the text. Then write a green word or phrase in each space to complete the dictionary entries.

Charles Dickens was a great English novelist. He published many famous books in his lifetime, and was working on *The Mystery of Edwin Drood* at the time of his death. A lot of Dickens's works have titles that are names – *Oliver Twist*, *Martin Chuzzlewit*, *Nicholas Nickleby*. Some critics call these 'rites of passage' novels because they tell the story of one person's journey through life – childhood, marriage, old age. Many of Dickens's novels contain social comment about the world and, in particular, the life of poor people in his day.

There have been many biographies of Dickens, but he never produced an autobiography. The closest we have to Dickens's story of his own life is the novel *David Copperfield*.

event *(n)*

origin *(n)*

plot *(n)*

source *(n)*

theme *(n)*

autobiography *(n)*

biography *(n)*

critic *(n)*

novelist *(n)*

publish *(v)*

rites of passage *(n)*

social comment *(n)*

work *(n)* (= piece of art or literature)

_____ a person who writes about art or literature and says whether it is good or bad

_____ a person who writes novels, i.e., stories about fictional characters

_____ any piece of art or literature, e.g., a painting, a novel, a play

_____ saying something (usually bad) about society; a play or novel of ~ sets out to tell people about a problem in society

_____ the important events in a person's life that form their character; a ~ novel tells the story of one person's struggle through life; the main ~ are adolescence, marriage, having children and the deaths of your parents

_____ the story of a real person's life, written by another person

_____ the story of a real person's life, written by the person him or herself

C Discuss these questions.

1 Do you know any novels that are rites of passage works?

2 Do you know any novels that contain social comment?

3 Have you ever read a biography?

4 What about an autobiography?

5 Whose life would you like to read about?

6 Do you think we need critics – or should we make up our own minds?

_____ to print and distribute a book, newspaper or magazine

Lesson 2: Reading

A Novelists are sometimes given the advice: 'Write about what you know!'
  1 Why is this good advice?
  2 What events from your life could you put in a novel?
  3 Which people from your life would make interesting characters?

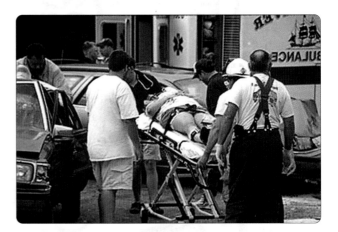

B Imagine you have this assignment (right).
  1 How could you carry out the necessary research?
  2 You have found a short biography of Charles Dickens. What information in the biography are you interested in, on this occasion?

C You have learnt a lot of reading skills in this course so far.
  1 Look at the Skills Check reminders. If you can't remember a particular point, refer back to the relevant page.
  2 The sentences in the yellow box are from a short biography of Charles Dickens. Match each sentence to one of the Skills Check reminders. (Clue: the **bold words** should help you!)
  3 Explain the meaning of each sentence in pairs.

  a The experience **clearly** affected his views on social reform.
  b In *Nicholas Nickelby*, **which** was published in instalments in 1838 and 1839, Dickens tells the story of a young man's struggles to make his way in the world.
  c He learnt **shorthand**, which is a quick way of taking notes from spoken language.
  d **He was put** into Marshalsea Prison.
  e His father, John Dickens, was a government clerk, **working** for the Royal Navy.
  f His mother found him a job in a factory, **located** on the banks of the River Thames.
  g In the same year, **he married Catherine**, who was the daughter of his friend …
  h John Dickens had a small collection of books, kept in the **attic** …
  i The **unfinished** novel, *The Mystery Of Edwin Drood*, was published in 1870.
  j This success **probably** led him to write his first novel, *The Pickwick Papers*, …

Greenhill College

Faculty: Arts   Semester 3

Assignment 5

In what ways did the life of Charles Dickens influence his literary works, particularly *David Copperfield?*

Skills Check

Reminders

Skill	Page
Confirming **precise meaning**	13
Understanding **negative prefixes**	14
Recognising **supposition**	17
Finding information in **active sentences**	21
Finding information in **passive sentences**	25
Looking for **internal definitions**	25
Understanding **non-finite clause**	29
Understanding *which / who / that* **clauses**	33
Understanding the **writer's attitude**	34

D Read the biography of Dickens on pages 34 and 35 of the Reading Resources book. Which events in his own life did Dickens probably use in his novels? Make a list of points.

Lesson 3: Learning new skills

Ⓐ From the evidence in the biography (Lesson 2), how do you think Charles Dickens felt about his mother and his father?

Ⓑ Look again at the biography of Charles Dickens. (Reading Resources book pages 34 and 35) and at the words in the green box. Work in pairs.
Student A: Find and underline the words in the **left** column.
Student B: Find and underline the words in the **right** column.
1 Guess the meaning from context.
2 Check the precise meaning in a dictionary if you need to.
3 Tell your partner about your words.

Ⓒ Continue working in pairs. Look at the participles in the blue box.
Student A: Find and circle in the text the participles in the **right** column.
Student B: Find and circle in the text the participles in the **left** column.
1 What is the subject of each participle?
2 What was the original tense of each participle?
3 Tell your partner about your participles.

Ⓓ Study this sentence from the text.

Then, in 1824, when Charles was only 12, his father's financial troubles finally caught up with him and he was imprisoned for debt.

1 What does this sentence tell you about the law in England in Dickens's time?
2 Read the Skills Check and check.
3 Read the statements in the yellow box about English society in Dickens's time. Find evidence in the text for each of the statements.

- Children did not have to go to school.
- You had to pay for schooling.
- Children could work in factories.
- Anyone could start a school, anywhere.
- Families could live together in prison.

A young Charles Dickens

transferred	trials
attic	portrays
imprisoned	instalments
pawn	struggles
banks	boarding school
polish	publicity
reform	serialisation
inherited	unfinished

working	earning
kept	leaving
including	learning
located	including
putting	telling
making	set

Skills Check

Making inferences about background knowledge

Dickens lived nearly 200 years ago in a different country from yours. Therefore, the society he lived in was probably very different from your society. Writers may not always explain the differences in a case like this. You may have to infer information.

Example:

in the text	we can infer ...
he was imprisoned for debt	you could go to prison for debt in England at the time of Dickens

Lesson 4: Applying new skills

(A) How can we infer each of the statements in the yellow box? Find evidence in the biography of Dickens on pages 34 and 35 of the Reading Resources book.

(B) You are going to read some extracts from *David Copperfield*.

  1 What is special about this novel, according to the biography of Dickens?

  2 What do you expect to find in *David Copperfield,* based on your answer to B1 above?

(C) You are going to look for events and characters from Dickens's real life in his novel *David Copperfield*.

  1 Find the list that you made in Lesson 2 Exercise D.

  2 Read the extracts from the novel on pages 36 and 37 of the Reading Resources book. Match real events and events in David Copperfield's life. Guess new words from context or ignore them on this occasion.

  3 Read the short essay from a critic (right). Tick the points that you noticed.

(D) Read the extracts from *David Copperfield* again. True or false?

  1 Mr Murdstone is David's stepfather.

  2 David is proud of his own abilities.

  3 Murdstone and Grinby's is a frightening place for a little boy.

  4 David has to check the bottles, then rinse and wash them.

  5 Mr Micawber is thin and bald.

  6 David goes to live with the Micawbers.

  7 Young ladies come at all hours for lessons with Mrs Micawber.

  8 David was probably paid on a Saturday.

(E) Would you like to read the novel *David Copperfield*? Why (not)?

- Dickens was very unhappy with his parents for sending him out to work.
- John Dickens's mother died in around 1825.
- Dickens's later novels didn't appear in instalments.
- Dickens didn't write an autobiography.
- Dickens was still writing at the time of his death.

CLASSIC REVIEW   *Issue 45*

There are many autobiographical details in *David Copperfield*.

Firstly, Dickens describes David's removal from school to work in a bottle factory, putting labels on the bottles, for six shillings a week. Dickens, of course, was removed from school to work in Warren's shoe polish factory, putting labels on the bottles of polish for the same salary. Like Murdstone and Grinby, Warren's was located near the River Thames.

Secondly, Charles had to go out to work because his father was in prison for debt. In David's case, he has to go out to work because his mother dies. Is Dickens saying his mother died for him in some way when she agreed to him going out to work? In the novel, Charles presents his parents as Mr and Mrs Micawber. He tells of Mrs Micawber trying, unsuccessfully, to start a school, as his own mother did, and of having to pawn things for the Micawbers, including books, as he had to do for his parents.

Finally, some critics have even mentioned that the initials of Dickens and his most famous hero are the same. Did CD become DC?

16

ball game *(n)*

court *(n)*

kick *(v)*

net *(n)*

pass *(v)*

playing field *(n)*

post *(n)*

rule *(n)*

team *(n)*

art gallery *(n)*

cinema *(n)*

concert *(n)*

cycling *(n)*

fishing *(n)*

fitness activity *(n)*

heritage site *(n)*

hobby *(n)*

sailing *(n)*

stadium *(n)*

swimming pool *(n)*

theatre *(n)*

theme park *(n)*

In this theme you are going to read tables and figures – graphs and pie charts.

Lesson 1: Vocabulary

You are going to learn some vocabulary to help you understand the tables and figures.

A Describe a ball game from your country. Use some of the red words.

B Look at the locations and activities in the pictures.
1 Label the pictures with the green words. Use a dictionary to check.
2 Number the locations and activities according to your personal preferences.

C Look at Table 1.
1 What is the table about?
2 Complete the *Activities* with some of the green words. Make any necessary changes.
3 What exactly does each figure in columns 2 and 3 represent? e.g., *64*.
4 Where does this information come from?
5 What other information would help you to evaluate this table?

D How could you show this information in a better way?
1 Discuss in pairs, then read the Skills Check.
2 What were the biggest changes in popularity between 2000 and 2001?

Table 1: Most popular outdoor activities (UK)

Activities	2000	2001
1 Walking	64	65
2 Visiting _____ sites – e.g., *old buildings*	27	28
3 Swimming in _____ or in the sea	25	25
4 Visiting art _____	19	21
5 Going to the _____	17	18
6 Doing a _____ – e.g., bird-watching	16	17
7 Going to a music _____	14	13
8 Visiting a _____ park	12	12
9 Going to the _____	10	11
10 _____ (inc. motorboats)	7	8
11 _____ (sea and river)	8	8
12 _____ (inc. sports and touring)	7	7
13 Health / _____ activities	5	6
14 Golf	5	5
15 Watching any sport, i.e., at a _____	5	4

Source: National Statistics Office
Note: Each figure represents the percentage of people who made at least one trip for this purpose in the year, e.g., 64% of people questioned said they went walking for pleasure in 2000.

Skills Check

Understanding statistics: Tables

Tables show **actual figures**. However, they are hard to read, and it is easy to miss important information.

Tips:
1 Turn the figures into a **line graph**, a **bar graph** or a **pie chart**.
2 Work out **percentages**.

Lesson 2: Reading

A What can you see …
1 at a cinema?
2 at the seaside?
3 at a theatre?
4 at a concert?
5 in an art gallery?
6 in a theme park?
7 at a health club?
8 at a swimming pool?
9 at a heritage site?
10 at a stadium?

B Imagine you are a student in the Faculty of Sports and Leisure Management at Greenhill College. Read the *Background* section on the handout and answer the questions.
1 What are the conditions for people to take part in outdoor leisure activities?
2 Why didn't poor people in the UK take part in outdoor leisure activities in the past?
3 What about rich people?
4 Why do some people with money, time and transport not take part in outdoor leisure activities today?

C What is the most popular leisure activity in the UK – reading or walking? Explain your answer.

D Read *The Assignment*.
1 What information about the UK do you know already that will help you answer one of the questions?
2 What information about the UK would be helpful in your research for each of the other questions?
3 What words could you type into a search engine to find that information?

E Imagine you have found the information about the UK on pages 38 and 39 of the Reading Resources book.
Which tables and / or figures help you answer each question in *The Assignment*?

F Which figures and tables would look similar in your country?

Greenhill College

Faculty: Sports and Leisure Management

Topic: *The Rise of Leisure*

Background

There are four necessary conditions for people to take part in outdoor leisure activities. They must have the time, the money and a method of transport to the location. They must also have the interest to spend the time and money.

In the past in the UK, many people could not take part in outdoor leisure activities, even if they had the interest. The working day was long, and there was little or no time off at the weekend. When people got a day off for a religious festival, they usually had no money for leisure activities. Only the rich could afford the time and money for such pleasures, and even they often stayed at home because transport was so bad.

Nowadays, most people in the UK have enough time and money for outdoor leisure activities. Transport links are good, although there are often traffic jams at holiday periods and the railways are getting a bad reputation for reliability.

Time, money and transport, therefore, are not a problem for most people. However, many people in the UK have no interest in outdoor activities. The most popular leisure activity in the UK, for example, for both men and women, is reading, followed closely by watching television.

The Assignment

Do some research into the situation in the UK by 2020. Try to answer the following questions:
1. Will people have more **time** for leisure activities?
2. Will people have the **money** for more leisure activities?
3. Will **transport** be available to the locations of outdoor leisure activities?
4. Will people have the **interest** to take part in such activities?

Lesson 3: Learning new skills

A Match the words and definitions from the figures and tables in Lesson 2.

1	axis	*a person who works from home*
2	scale	*available to be used*
3	unit of measurement	*division of information into sections*
4	breakdown	*moving into or out of a country*
5	commuting	*percentage of something*
6	disposable	*the general direction of something*
7	estimated	*the horizontal and vertical lines on a graph*
8	migration	*the meanings of numbers on the y (or vertical) axis*
9	proportion	*the real item that the scale refers to, e.g., people, dollars*
10	source	*travelling to and from work every day*
11	teleworker	*where information comes from*
12	trend	*worked out from information but not necessarily accurate*

B Read Skills Check 1. Then study the graphs on pages 38 and 39 of the Reading Resources book and answer each of the questions in the Skills Check.

C Read Skills Checks 2 and 3. Then follow each tip.

D What will the statistics be in 2020 for each of the following areas? Use the information from the graphs to make predictions.

1 disposable income (as a percentage of 1971)
2 people working more than 45 hours per week (as a percentage of 1997)
3 number of teleworkers
4 proportion of men aged 50–64 in paid employment
5 effect of #2 and #3 above on main weekly activities (Table 1)

E What will be the effect on leisure activities of your predictions from Exercise D?

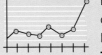

Lesson 4: Applying new skills

Figure 1: Cinema visits in the UK

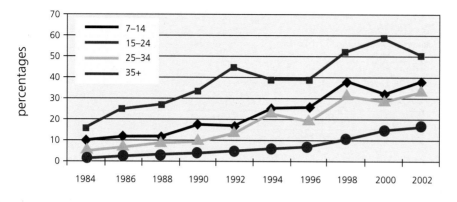

Cinema visits by age group

Source: National Statistics Office

Note: Figures represent percentage in age group who made at least one cinema visit a month in the previous year.

A Read Figure 1 and answer the questions.
1 What has happened to cinema visits in the UK in general in the last 20 years?
2 What exactly does the figure of *10* for the 7–14 age group mean?
3 What is the trend for the 35+ age group?
4 What will the figure be for the 25–34 age group in 2020?
5 What may be the reasons for this data?
6 Are you surprised by any of this data? Why (not)?

B You have another assignment about leisure management. Read the *Background* section on the handout. True or false?
1 Circuses are outdoor leisure activities.
2 People still want their governments to provide circuses.
3 It takes a long time to provide facilities for outdoor leisure activities.

C Read *The Assignment*.
1 What information about the UK do you know already that will help you?
2 What information about the UK would be helpful in your research?
3 What words could you type into a search engine to find that information?

D Imagine that you have found the information on pages 40 and 41 of the Reading Resources book. Read the tables and figures and do the assignment.

Greenhill College

Faculty: Sports and Leisure Management

Topic: *Predict and Provide*

Background

The Roman poet Juvenal, who lived from 55 CE to 127 CE, said that the people of Rome only demanded two things from their rulers – bread and circuses. Both were needed for life – people needed to eat to sustain the body and to visit the circus for pleasure.

People still demand 'bread and circuses' from their governments, although both have become more sophisticated. In the case of the 'circuses', people demand access to outdoor leisure facilities of all kinds.

A national government must **predict** demand for different types of outdoor leisure activities, and **provide** the appropriate facilities. In some cases, it takes years to build facilities and the transport infrastructure, so national governments must use current statistics to predict the situation in 20 or even 50 years' time.

The Assignment

1. Do some research into outdoor leisure activities in the UK.
2. Predict changes in outdoor activities by the year 2020.
3. Make a list of facilities the British Government should consider providing.

In this theme you are going to read two leaflets about exercise.

Lesson 1: Vocabulary

You are going to learn some vocabulary that you will need to understand the leaflets.

Ⓐ Work in pairs.

Student A: Read Text 1. **Student B**: Read Text 2.

1 Complete your text with a red word in each space. Make any necessary changes.

2 Make notes of the important information.

3 Close your books and explain the information in your text to your partner.

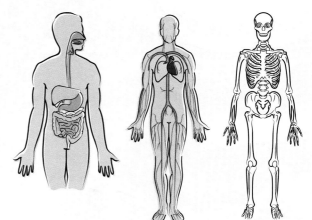

Text 1

Fast food, like burgers and sweet snacks, is becoming more and more popular. This kind of food gives us quick _____ from the _____ and carbohydrate, but it is not very good for us.

Firstly, many fast foods contain a large amount of _____. We need this in our food, but *vegetable* fat is better than the *animal* fat in many fast foods. Chips are just potatoes fried in _____.

Secondly, many fast foods contain a lot of salt (NaCl). We need some _____ like salt, but too much causes problems.

Finally, sweet snacks contain a lot of sugar, which is not bad in small amounts, but too much can make you _____.

Text 2

The human body needs _____ every day. It makes the _____ work, which helps us to live and move.

We get the energy from protein and _____ in our food. _____ comes, for example, from fish and meat, while carbohydrate comes from foods like bread, rice and pasta.

We also need some _____ in our food to help with digestion in the stomach. We get it from fruit and vegetables and from cereals.

Finally, we need a small amount of vitamins and _____ to keep us healthy. The main vitamin (C) is from fruit like oranges.

carbohydrate *(n)*
energy *(n)*
fat *(adj)*
fat/s *(n)*
fibre *(n)*
mineral *(n)*
muscles *(n)*
protein *(n)*
vitamin *(n)*
blood *(n)*
bone *(n)*
exercise *(n)*
fit *(adj)*
fitness *(n)*
heart *(n)*
hip *(n)*
lung *(n)*
neck *(n)*
spine *(n)*

Ⓑ Look at the diagrams.

1 Label them with green words. Use a dictionary to check your answers.

2 Do you know the names of any other parts of the body? Add labels.

Ⓒ Discuss in groups.

1 Are you fit?

2 Were you fitter when you were younger?

3 How can you get fit?

4 Is fitness important?

Lesson 2: Reading review (1)

A In this course you have learnt how to deal with a new word or phrase. You have learnt to look for an internal definition, or, if there isn't one, to guess then check the precise meaning with a dictionary if necessary.

1 Look at the words and phrases in the yellow box. Do you understand any of them?

2 Read *What is exercise?* on pages 42 and 43 of the Reading Resources book. Deal with the words and phrases as you meet them in the text.

stretching	heart rate	stationary
muscle strain	blood pressure	aerobics
tear (rhymes with *wear*)	cardiovascular	contraction
aerobic exercise	jogging	circulatory system
oxygen	skipping	criteria

B Answer these questions about the information in *What is exercise?*

1 What are the three basic types of exercise?

2 Which parts of the body are involved in each type?

3 Which type of exercise should you always do? Why?

4 What criteria must any exercise programme meet?

C In this course you have learnt to find the main point of a text. Look at *How much exercise is necessary?* What is the main point of this text?

D In this course you have learnt to find the main point of a sentence by ignoring extra information. Read these sentences from *How much exercise is necessary?* Cross out the extra information that you don't need to get the main point in each case.

1 Firstly, people who do not take regular exercise are about seven times more likely to suffer a stroke.

2 In addition, exercise increases blood volume, which reduces the lipidity or 'fattiness' of the blood.

3 Long-distance runners, for example, can have as much as a litre more blood than the average person.

4 Of course, the best-known effect of exercise is weight loss, because exercise makes muscles hungry for fat, which they need for fuel.

5 In addition, a recent study at the Tufts University, which is in Massachusetts, has shown that exercise also increases the metabolic rate (the speed at which your body as a whole works).

E Read *How much exercise is necessary?* Find, as quickly as possible:

1 the main point of the text.

2 the main points of each sentence.

F In this course you have learnt to recognise negative prefixes. Read *What is the best exercise programme for me?*

1 Make a list of words with negative prefixes.

2 Work out the meaning of each one from context if possible. If not, look up the positive word in a dictionary.

G Work in groups. Discuss these questions.

1 Do *you* need to start a regular exercise programme? Why (not)?

2 If so, which type of exercise would you like to start doing? When?

Lesson 3: Reading review (2)

A The text on the right is from the first draft of a leaflet produced by Greenhill College Sports and Fitness Centre. Look quickly at the topic sentences in the text. What is the text about?

B In this course you have learnt to recognise extra information in a clause starting with a participle (-*ing* or -*ed*).

1 The writer of the Pilates text wants to add some extra information. Decide where each phrase in the blue box should go. Sometimes the extra information is an internal definition.

2 Check with the text on pages 42 and 43 of the Reading Resources book.

> - determined to strengthen his body
> - developed in the 1920s by Joseph Pilates
> - disabled by their wounds
> - explaining the principles of control over muscles
> - straightening the spine
> - meaning the abdominal muscles in the stomach
> - moving to England in 1912
> - which most of them do not have
> - opening a fitness centre there
> - using this special equipment
> - caused by a deficiency of vitamin D
> - writing just before the Second World War
> - including springs attached to beds

C In this course you have learnt how to recognise the writer's attitude to information in a text. Find one piece of information which the writer thinks …

1 is true.
2 is probably true.
3 may be true.
4 may be a myth.

D Work in pairs. Test each other on the information about Pilates and his exercise method.

PILATES is a 'stretch and strengthen' exercise type, … The programme was originally designed for dancers, but it is now becoming popular with all types of people, because it clearly has many health benefits.

The Pilates method focuses on breathing and working muscles from the inside to strengthen your core, …, the hips and the lower back. There is evidence that Pilates helps to improve posture, …

Joseph H Pilates was born in 1880, in Germany. In his childhood, it seems that he suffered from rickets, which is a disease of the bones … As he grew up, he studied yoga and exercises from Ancient Greece and Rome, … He became a skier and gymnast and … worked as a boxer and circus performer.

During the First World War, he was interned, serving as an orderly, or cleaner, in a hospital, where he met soldiers … He began to produce special equipment to assist recovery, … It is said that patients recovered more quickly when they exercised …

After the war, Joseph moved back to Germany, but emigrated to the US when the army called him up to train soldiers. He settled in New York,… Presumably, he helped at least one famous person, because his centre was soon used by the rich and famous of the day.

He wrote several books about his system, …In his books, he made big claims for the power of exercise, …:

"The lack of knowledge of general health on the people's part is largely responsible for world conditions today, responsible for combat, discouragement, crime and premature death, because a healthy body, …, makes for a clean and healthy mind."

J Pilates, 1939

Pilates died in 1967.

Lesson 4: Reading review (3)

A Match words from each column to make phrases from the texts in Lessons 2 and 3. Find the phrases in the texts and check your answers.

1 heart	activity
2 blood	exercise
3 muscle	lifestyle
4 aerobic	loss
5 exercise	pressure
6 physical	profession
7 circulatory	programme
8 active	rate
9 weight	strain
10 medical	system

B Choose a preposition / particle from the yellow box to complete each verb from the text in Lessons 2 and 3. You can only use each word once.

about   around   back   down   from   in   into   on   out   over   to   up

1 build	**5** divide	**9** carry
2 cool	**6** come	**10** worry
3 rush	**7** compare	**11** settle
4 depend	**8** spread	**12** move

C You are going to read part of the final version of the leaflet from Greenhill College Sports and Fitness Club (Lesson 3) on pages 44 and 45 of the Reading Resources book.
Work in groups of three.
Student A: Read about yoga.
Student B: Read about t'ai chi.
Student C: Read about the Alexander Technique.
Find out and make notes of:
1 the main factual information in your text concerning:
  • the benefits of the exercise type.
  • the inventor or inventors.
2 the attitude of the writer to information in your text.
3 any important points regarding this exercise type at Greenhill College Sports and Fitness Club.
As you read, deal with any new words and phrases, making a note of the internal definitions, your guesswork or the dictionary definition that you found.

D Work in the same groups of three.
Close your Reading Resources book. Give important information from your text to the two people in your group. Explain the meaning of new words and phrases as necessary.

E Continue in your groups of three. Imagine that you have decided to enrol at the college fitness club. Try to decide which exercise type to join – yoga, t'ai chi or the Alexander Technique.

THEME 1
Education, Teaching and Learning

brain (n)

forget (v)

memory (n)

remember (v)

revise (v)

achieve (v)

assess (v)

knowledge (n)

skill (n)

training (n)

THEME 2
Daily Life, Nature … or Nurture?

adult (n)

child/ren (n)

husband (n)

parent (n)

relationship (n)

response (n)

wife (n)

affect (v)

bring up (v)

environment (n)

factor (n)

genes (n)

genetics (n)

inherit (v)

THEME 3
Work and Business, SOMething to Live For

acronym (n)

applicant (n)

decide (v)

evaluate (v)

generate (v)

imagine (v)

process (n)

select (v)

solution (n)

colleague (n)

flexible (adj)

overtime (n)

promotion (n)

salary (n)

secure (adj)

security (n)

THEME 4
Science and Nature, Forecasting the Weather

climate (n)

desert (n)

living thing (n)

plant (n)

polar (adj)

tropical (adj)

collect (v)

conclude (v)

measure (v)

observe (v)

predict (v)

THEME 5
The Physical World, Black Gold

area *(n)*

border *(v)*

industry *(n)*

natural feature *(n)*

neighbour *(n)*

population *(n)*

drill *(v)*

energy *(n)*

form *(v)*

fuel *(n)*

geologist *(n)*

petroleum *(n)*

plastic *(n)*

run out *(v)*

source *(n)*

surface *(n)*

underground *(adj)*

well *(n)*

THEME 6
Culture and Civilization, Twenty-Six Civilizations

bride *(n)*

ceremony *(n)*

groom *(n)*

marriage *(n)*

marry *(v)*

reception *(n)*

relative *(n)*

wedding *(n)*

architecture *(n)*

agriculture *(n)*

government *(n)*

law *(n)*

religion *(n)*

technology *(n)*

the arts *(n)*

THEME 7
They Made Our World, Preserving Food

device *(n)*

experiment *(v)*

invent *(v)*

invention *(n)*

inventor *(n)*

laboratory *(n)*

materials *(n)*

patent *(n)*

telegraph *(n)*

bacteria *(n)*

disease *(n)*

drug *(n)*

food preservation *(n)*

infect *(v)*

infection *(n)*

substance *(n)*

THEME 8
Art and Literature, Dickens and *David Copperfield*

event *(n)*

origin *(n)*

plot *(n)*

source *(n)*

theme *(n)*

autobiography *(n)*

biography *(n)*

critic *(n)*

novelist *(n)*

publish *(v)*

rites of passage *(n)*

social comment *(n)*

work *(n)* (= piece of art or literature)

THEME 9
Sports and Leisure, Predict and Provide

ball game (n)

court (n)

kick (v)

net (n)

pass (v)

playing field (n)

post (n)

rule (n)

team (n)

art gallery (n)

cinema (n)

concert (n)

cycling (n)

fishing (n)

fitness activity (n)

heritage site (n)

hobby (n)

sailing (n)

stadium (n)

swimming pool (n)

theatre (n)

theme park (n)

THEME 10
Nutrition and Health, Love Your Heart

carbohydrate (n)

energy (n)

fat (adj)

fat/s (n)

fibre (n)

mineral (n)

muscles (n)

protein (n)

vitamin (n)

blood (n)

bone (n)

exercise (n)

fit (adj)

fitness (n)

heart (n)

hip (n)

lung (n)

neck (n)

spine (n)

---

achieve (v)

acronym (n)

adult (n)

affect (v)

agriculture (n)

applicant (n)

architecture (n)

area (n)

art gallery (n)

assess (v)

autobiography (n)

bacteria (n)

ball game (n)

biography (n)

blood (n)

bone (n)

border (v)

brain (n)

bride (n)

bring up (v)

carbohydrate (n)

ceremony (n)

child/ren (n)

cinema (n)

climate (n)

colleague (n)

---

collect (v)

concert (n)

conclude (v)

court (n)

critic (n)

cycling (n)

decide (v)

desert (n)

device (n)

disease (n)

drill (v)

drug (n)

energy (n)

energy (n)

environment (n)

evaluate (v)

event (n)

exercise (n)

experiment (v)

factor (n)

fat (adj)

fat/s (n)

fibre (n)

fishing (n)

fit (adj)

fitness (n)

fitness activity (n)

flexible (adj)

food preservation (n)

forget (v)

form (v)

fuel (n)

generate (v)

genes (n)

genetics (n)

geologist (n)

government (n)

groom (n)

heart (n)

heritage site (n)

hip (n)

hobby (n)

husband (n)

imagine (v)

industry (n)

infect (v)

infection (n)

inherit (v)

invent (v)

invention (n)

inventor (n)

kick (v)

knowledge (n)

laboratory (n)

law (n)

living thing (n)

lung (n)

marriage (n)

marry (v)

materials (n)

measure (v)

memory (n)

mineral (n)

muscles (n)

natural feature (n)

neck (n)

neighbour (n)

net (n)

novelist (n)

observe (v)

origin (n)

overtime (n)

parent (n)

pass (v)

patent (n)

petroleum (n)

plant (n)

plastic (n)

playing field (n)

plot (n)

polar (adj)

population (n)

post (n)

predict (v)

process (n)

promotion (n)

protein (n)

publish (v)

reception (n)

relationship (n)

relative (n)

religion (n)

remember (v)

response (n)

revise (v)

rites of passage (n)

rule (n)

run out (v)

sailing (n)

salary (n)

secure (adj)

security (n)

select (v)

skill (n)

social comment (n)

solution (n)

source (n)

source (n)

spine (n)

stadium (n)

substance (n)

surface (n)

swimming pool (n)

team (n)

technology (n)

telegraph (n)

the arts (n)

theatre (n)

theme (n)

theme park (n)

training (n)

tropical (adj)

underground (adj)

vitamin (n)

wedding (n)

well (n)

wife (n)

work (n) (= piece of art or literature)